A TREATISE ON STARS

Also by Mei-mei Berssenbrugge

The Lit Cloud (with Kiki Smith)
Hello, the Roses
I Love Artists: New and Selected Poems
Concordance (with Kiki Smith)
Nest
Four Year Old Girl
Endocrinology (with Kiki Smith)
Sphericity (with Richard Tuttle)
Hiddenness (with Richard Tuttle)
Empathy
The Heat Bird
Random Possession
Summits Move with the Tide

A TREATISE ON STARS

MEI-MEI BERSSENBRUGGE

A New Directions Book

Manufactured in the United States of America
New Directions Books are printed on acid-free paper
First published as a New Directions Paperbook (NDP1469) in 2020
Design by Eileen Bellamy

Library of Congress Cataloging-in-Publication Data
Names: Berssenbrugge, Mei-mei, author.
Title: A Treatise on Stars / Mei-mei Berssenbrugge.
Description: First edition. | New York: New Directions Books, 2020. | "A New Directions book."
Identifiers: LCCN 2019047008 | ISBN 9780811229388 (paperback; alk. paper) | ISBN 9780811229395 (ebook)
Subjects: LCGFT: Poetry.
Classification: LCC PS3552.E77 T74 2020 | DDC 811/.54—dc23
LC record available at https://lccn.loc.gov/2019047008

10 9 8 7 6 5 4 3 2

New Directions Books are published for James Laughlin
by New Directions Publishing Corporation
80 Eighth Avenue, New York 10011
ndbooks.com

to Richard and Martha

CONTENTS

I

II

I

STAR BEINGS

1

In late afternoon, stars are not visible.

Everything arrives energetically, at first.

I wait to see what I'll recognize, as diffuse sky resolves into points of light and glitter.

When Venus appears, objects are just visible; silhouettes seem larger, nearer; voices are audible at a distance, though words don't make precise sense.

Glancing to the right of Antares in medium blue, I intuit cosmic allurement.

Stars arrive non-visually, first.

I practice to see light in this process of evanescence, like an aroma.

The field of heaven, which operates outside space-time, is formed by acts of other entities, other stars, and by people who rise in the dark to look for them and place them.

When mind extends toward sky, it may take the form of a perceived star, because respect is a portal.

When your experience ardently links to an object or person where you live—husband, tree, stone—you try to hold onto the visibility of this object and its location.

Connecting with a geography of sky gives this sense of security, inspiration.

I ally with a crater on the plain, also the comet's light.

2

Venus arrives in cerulean; Antares, second star is just visible, then Pico in indigo.

Full dark: light streaks from one star to another like communication, travel.

Planets line up and turn with their DNA, energy around them, like a web struck by light.

Stars are holes in the dark; when I look at one, I go there; entity contact eases emotion.

I ask heaven that we be left with some essence of what has disappeared, that one day we again experience physical beauties no longer seen.

Remembering concentrates something at work in the present; visibility is like memory, dimensions also; invisible, organizing substrates unify past and present.

They provide a framework that keeps stars in place, cohering the dynamic quanta of infinity, so travel is easy.

This frame does not emit light, nor other waves, nor show itself by absorbing light from hot dust or star death, as with a concentrating black hole, nor show how far we extend into its ecology.

Watching is like living on the mesa, while deepening my reception to it.

Richness I concentrate is not contained; I radiate desert fragrance spontaneously from a wild rose in my dream.

May we go to that time; I mean, we'll all see the beginning.

3

She passed on her observations of Venus and spring dawn.

We did not ask the personal details of her study.

We thought, naturally, object and subject processes connect, that night sky and knowing are undivided.

Perhaps creativity is the unfoldment of relations between objective and emotion in space.

The beingness of stars onto which my consciousness projects awe is also consciousness as light.

When we expand into any unknown, we use the term origin, i.e., one time.

Waiting for stars I know is the fullness of time, contingent time.

I go out before dawn to check Venus on my birthday.

I feel extension, pre-space through which dawn will arrive.

There's an ambience of bird song, cicadas.

I aspire for transparent space to diffuse dissonance inside me to its quantum complement; sky lightens.

4

I see a white tree against black ground.

Its shape is a person reaching up with wide arms, but fuzzy in outline from leaves and blossoms.

I study how gravity, allure, origin create the shape.

Natural law is represented by the dark from which my tree grows.

Night elicits, then highlights the tree, as if brightness (day, experience) were a flexible substance being thought into coherence, a mold.

Night is of day, as day is transparent, as dark energy is of light attraction.

The tree attains its most intimate relation with black ground in the context of my viewing.

I perceive the beingness of stars as a kind of visually emotive flow-through.

A woman watching is like a mirror surface on the outermost layer of appearance or her experience of the tree.

Each of us when we look at stars is the localized reflection.

I went out with him to see the Spiral branching away.

It viscerally enmeshes us in subtle fields of other beings thinking through space in lines of light.

Distance between viewer and star resolves into one experience, point or singularity.

As you continually generate the transparency of flowing space, it must continually unfold matter that shines.

CONSCIOUSNESS SELF-LEARNS

1

Plants and rocks lay under night sky; ground is a subject of sky; the relation's a force.

I combine descriptions with ideas of forces; my photograph of night sky's like a text of symbols.

Look inside when you are struggling; every cell in your body emits light.

Cilia beat rhythms into space, signaling cells of wildflowers in a field, signaling sky.

I connect to it, holding the hand of our friend, who's sleeping.

When I look at a constellation, I construct lines from indivisible points, bind seeing to an infinity of points and single brights, at the same time.

I may not recall these thoughts tomorrow, and I'm anxious, as if stars had extinguished.

Then, talking to you about his illness provokes tension, disagreement that stirs in my memory lost thoughts.

Our difference became a permeable membrane between each person and the whole.

Even though my mind focused within bounds, it's indivisible from sky I see, because seeing is as a field.

Looking is an innate impulse toward wholeness.

2

Particles flash in and out of being; the border between life and death may not continue in other dimensions; gravity and time flex.

Struggle and freedom elide.

When you arrive at my house ill, I throw my arms around you and lead you to a chair, "What happened?"

"I'm glad your mind is clear, even with such pain;" I place my hand on your chest and pray.

And I pray when I read the paper, for lost people.

Any transformation is an expressive aspect of this intent.

World is undivided, observer and observed, as particle from its wave nature, as prayer from a compassionate outcome, when prayer is multiplied.

Next week, you find me crying over a fawn whose mother was killed; I drove to town for milk, but when I returned the fawn had died.

"It was very hungry, now it's dead," I tell you; "Its mind flows into my mind."

"I'm weeping because I want milk."

3

The dead fawn is a delicate, cosmic holding-position, like the invisible spiral around a crane circling the marsh to land.

Its pattern of being maintains without a fixed structure, whose virtual particles and fields may include my prayers, my compassion for it.

The way some waves continue into space when light and matter are removed, using a latent mentality outside space-time, my fervent plea may evolve physically.

From possibility, feeling for a faun generates photons like rain on matted fur; words, visions, images of milk engage with the baby for a better outcome.

When I recognize this, effects become intentional, hopeful, because love is a measurement.

4

I think waves that condense into particles retain their original information and that coherence among these waves is lost when an organism dies, like a person swept into the chaos of a party.

He can no longer hear himself or speak.

When no one observes us, not even ourselves, our particles regain their wave aspect.

Our attention that collapses quanta contains a kind of meaning intrinsic to feeling connected.

I sit on the patio and watch small birds calling, fluttering in the rain.

Our friend asks if I saw an oriole on the stones outside his window, but I did not.

Describing a bird you see, which I did not see, is part of collective consciousness self-learning.

Ghosts, angels, phantom birds, crop circles, even hoaxes incarnate some of this wholeness.

Connecting to it is being, wherein through prayer my consciousness binds with subtle energy of a bird I did not see?

Coda

I love a person leaving who sees birds in other worlds, nearby.

All the good in nature I imagine in birds, their images like quantum leaps.

Goodness is part of my awareness that sensing a bird intends.

We feel love shape a situation in which our friend's inseparable on a constitutive level from the immediate.

Worlds emerge and transform, so metaphor uses birds to extend disrupted thought.

I want to learn from what generated the metaphor, the need.

SCALAR

1

You can rise to a level of not knowing that's untouched by entropy.

Out of uncertainty, openness: order is maintained.

You rise to a realization beyond decay.

There's a deeper intelligence than that.

It radiates like light across a border between quanta and matter, unifying them.

Your physical body and your quantum body of probabilities are like two candles on a table.

Space between them evenly fills with photons of light, no separation at the particle level.

You carry one candle outside and hold it up against a background of stars.

Space between candle and a star fills with waves that bind them; each star's as connected to it as the one inside.

Look at your candle, then look at Sirius; photons from each hitting your retina electrochemically flash.

You're another flame or star in the surrounding interconnected field.

Yet, what is the structure of this connectedness?

The field is your light and not knowing simultaneously, local light.

You observe sky's dimensions according to our consensus on entropy.

You don't see the unifying factor in all things; you can't perceive the enfoldment of chance and fatigue.

2

Time also enfolds.

Your present state may not relate to what's past, but to a more fundamental structure, like a pool of widening rings from a stone.

This moment cuts through the physical universe now and seems to hold all of space in itself.

What happens today may be altered by an event in the future, since space consists of ambiguous, foggy regions, where a particle may pass on your last day.

Awareness creates the duration you experience.

If you try to divide duration, it's like suddenly passing a gold blade through the flame.

You divide space you think time occupies, not motion itself.

Imagine duration as non-referential time, change, and freedom from the decay inevitably implied.

You observe creative emergence.

Growth indicates intelligence of the universe as a whole in space you measure between heartbeats: new content, new time.

3

I can't distinguish duration that separates two instants from my memory that connects them.

Duration continues what has passed with now; it implies consciousness, for which time flows.

Brain steps down energy radiating from stars through optic nerve to pineal gland arranging these myriad photons into a neurological, space-time grid.

It conveys the influx of light as a field, mentality.

So thought is a form of organized light.

Non-physical variables, my wish, intent, expectance also create and transcribe energy.

Even if mind never operates as slowly as the speed of starlight, your future dwells gracefully in the space of your imagining.

4

A body or galaxy requires continuous energy to maintain, like a whirlpool in a fast stream.

Its spiral persists, though water constantly moves in and out of it.

A standing wave of photons comprises the immanent grid of starlight that permeates space; and vice versa, emanations from earth, sun, your nervousness and emotion radiate out.

You observe this enigmatic dark energy, where every point in space contains intersecting photons from every star, past and present.

Zero-sum, immense creativity streams through you, gyre of light as intelligence or your intent to observe.

The observation is grainy; people, dogs, trees are mosaics, a crystalline lattice of interacting bits; each "decides" countless times per second whether to leap to the next moment.

Light, information, so activated composes a body in the process of coalescence, outcrop of growing, infinite fields.

Nurture belief that your body's infused with the deep intelligence of this information, whose sole purpose is to sustain you.

5

Add to four dimensions inner space, mind, the virtual.

All objects connect, for example, through meaning in hyperspace.

Our plans for the future exist as images, and these cognitive structures are also in hyperspace, since mind is more like a spatial concept.

What we call star lines, like songs, ley lines are the interconnectivity.

There's no need to decide what's true; reality's a learning curve.

Then, he tells me about his pictures of stars and galaxies; he projects himself into space, taking with him a 35mm camera.

He puts the lens to his forehead and photographs the sun, moon, Milky Way, Andromeda.

He has many boxes of these images.

To commune, deepest process of space, evolves toward more connection, complexity.

When I look at night sky, I touch inner space with heaven; plasma streams across borders.

Time is not blankness through which light travels, more like plasma.

Consciousness embodies it by acting self-referentially, not dualistically as in seeing, not seeing.

Through emotional attraction, mass affinity, tachyonic speed, we know bodies and radiance are interwoven; what we call originary is instant.

THE LOOM

1

I would show her the night sky and point out certain stars.

A person, being of cosmic origin, can become one with a star.

Looking underlies unity between earth and sky.

Through black holes, UFOs, star beings, ETs, collective memory: night influences our DNA.

I point out the Loom; a small, white star is the crosspiece, brightness on depth granting shape and placement.

Pleiades, Andromeda, Aldebaran weave dimensions of dark, light, and the invisible.

Attention becomes thinking; feeling divines a precise order of reality in imaginal space.

We've greater power to participate in the rhythms of our place, enlivening a vertical, ideational channel, here to there, as perception, a kind of breath made of transparency.

2

In college, a young man took me to a hill near town to wait for star people, and I've continued looking for them.

From starlight I sense a pulse like breathing, but only the exhale of radiance to intensifying radiance as beauty.

I focus on meaning flowing through seeing to shape an entity; intrinsic meaning is explicitly realized as the beingness of light.

Birds, dolphins, whales use this more immediate, communicatory alignment with meaning as gestalt, song.

Their cosmic relations illuminate us through an invisible matrix that does not emit or reflect light, attached to earth as being, a kind of gravity in infinity.

I tell her Orion, Dog Star, Pleiades, Cassiopeia.

Their light and heat from our bodies commingle.

3

I point out the flyway of images rising and descending, like an axis, a tree, standing in our warm boots and jackets, absorbing data from above.

We've always used trees to organize intelligence, and you will climb one to know with others that matter emanates from it.

Its canopy spreads into the firmament to organize space-time, setting star fields in motion.

I tell you this upper world is real, experiential, conscious and accessible to us by our response, because ramification is within.

Your pulse aligns you with other light as a ladder of branches and leaves into heaven, with birds in the branches.

Your focus is aliveness with another; we look with analogue, textile eyes at the dark field, generative gravity of consciousness, and the field moves toward us.

It pulsates, as if potentia and subject were shapeshifting with earth.

At what point is an observation complete, if this consciousness is homogeneous, distributed?

Upper and lower branches entangle as reference, human culture.

Night situates within nested, self-organizing narratives that ascend, such as, I am your mother and consciousness is mother.

4

Sometimes I brought the ETs flowers, sometimes a pretty rock.

I tell her that rocks like meteorites retain light, a sensible energy thought into substance by experiencing it.

All life is this coherence of light being emitted and received, then sometimes thought.

By day, observation spreads out as waves; Milky Way is an invisible potential, and I can imagine a wave function for the universe.

Up to now cosmos manifested in fragments when observed by conscious beings.

Conscious beings are like the morphogenesis of a capacity or sphere, where cause doesn't exist.

Particles stream back and forth in narrative lines, and wonder as scale stabilizes our uncertainty by welcoming light, this state with enough new information for intelligence and enough ground for us.

Being is not the straight line a photon travels, but fractal, like the edge of a borealis.

Its locus is our recognition that ebbs and flows.

I transcribe a text, a weave that emits and reflects the light in which a universe less compatible would be invisible.

JAGUAR

1

People around Abiquiu claim descent from the Pleiadians and their beloved animals.

We've always known relatives from other places, Andromedans, Orionites, Zeta-reticulans, Sirians.

Cosmic relations are expressed by our plaza, also in new homes we align with winter and summer light.

All around are invisible realities where contact may occur.

Some hear coyotes speaking in computer beeps; some entertain guests unaware.

Owls, for example, have one song beyond the range of our hearing, interleaved with multi-dimensional information.

The 4D projection of this song generates a star.

I invite you to stand close tonight looking up, while our heart frequencies entrain, and we experience heart cognition, a kind of analytic thought oriented around images with feeling.

Associating memories attract light.

Your memory becomes an informational flow accessed through pathways or stories others share with others, that seem simple in daylight, though you may be traveling backward in time or forward by resonance into space.

That may be the only way to communicate with some others.

2

Where are you going? Where are you coming from?

I'm going to the stone circle at the end of my land; I'm going to collect seeds from primroses on the road, to look at some land to buy, to visit my friend, visit my mother.

Crossing and recrossing arroyos and mesas create a dense web between beings and home.

In the same way, the neural grid of an ecosystem continually adjusts to maintain, as light between the hearts of mother and daughter or light back and forth from stars maintains homeodynamics in space.

Our desire for light, for consciousness, is pulled from the transcendent domain of potentia by the needs of environment herself.

3

When you were a baby, my friend painted the star beings who visited her as angels, kachinas, very beautiful snakes.

She taught us to hold our connection with each other in a new geography that weaves stars with the ground.

Milky Way courses overhead; dark patches show against its foam, like divinations.

Earth is a node of intersections in our galaxy and beyond, receiving millions of tons of extraterrestrial material a year as cosmic dust, meteorites, asteroids breaking up to scatter their bacteria and splash ours back out.

All life forms are in potential genetic exchange; viruses transpose DNA between mosquitoes and humans, for example, or between plants and microorganisms from space.

We symbiotically merge into more complex new species in order to stabilize earth's self-organizing whole.

4

I describe consciousness as mother, earth, and the intelligence that shapes it.

It's like an image of the moon on two different television sets.

The real moon exists in different space than our living room.

When we go outside at night, I'm nervous; I'm afraid for the animals; I mix consciousness with time, confuse time with what could happen.

I struggle for understanding beyond environmental fears and grief.

Consciousness is like the live feed of a jaguar on two different video screens.

The real jaguar's filmed in a rainforest, preparing her energies.

Before, I knew what to look for at night; I no longer know.

My fear offers new possibility, the way awareness can create.

Two birds perch in a constellation tree with the same name; one eats starfruit; the other looks on.

They're together, which we recognize, like the sun and moon; one shines out; one waits for light.

Observing and observed universe are complementary aspects of their love.

THE PLEIADES

1

It's March; rain fills seven indentations in a large stone, like a table.

Then twilight, all is permeable, open to relation.

Then the Pleiades at night shine in collected rain; I open myself to receive their reflected light.

Starlight is so bright it seems dark to my unaccustomed eyes, as I enter into a closeness like disorientation.

So long as I feel my family around me, I haven't experienced oneness; it's difficult at night to hold onto self, when earth shifts through transformation.

Bright Pleiades circling night sky I address as sisters, kin, suggesting human form.

I refer more to relation than beings.

Everything seen establishes relation.

2

Before dawn on spring solstice, Pleiades appear at the horizon; Milky Way still spans east to west.

Then sunrise, Pleiades dim, and the moon pales.

Venus, morning star, comes running.

Each constellation represents meaning that is a being, and all beings connect, so sky has spiritual dimension.

Naming is part of this overall connection, consciousness; then we're more at ease with wonder.

Wonder is like dawn light, source before anything was manifest.

We gaze up into dark energy of great fluidity.

Perhaps words like being or spirit aren't accurate; even though I say, my sisters who rise at dawn, I mean presence as reciprocity.

3

I still recall the deep silence when I contacted my sister and agreed to work with her to construct a link between our family and the stars.

We ascend from imagining to the consciousness of each star we touch, in neither ordinary or non-ordinary reality.

It's a unified field, this darkness we acknowledge, so that consciousness may expand.

Pleiades at dawn signify beginning; multiple, synchronous relations evoke verbal from visual and vice versa.

A symbol gains power from such multiplicity.

Darkness enables us to cross the boundary of space-time to outer space, because the force of existence, what happens, evolution, flows through us as connection.

We accept our experience as an expression of this.

4

Some stars occupy two places in circular or permeable time; also, one star may have several aspects, evening as well.

I can depict a constellation in the calyx of a rose, but it's more accurate to portray source, relation.

I receive a word from a star, and I place it in my ordinary speech through the day, repeating the word, and the star materializes.

Days later, Pleiades stay below at dawn.

Our observation deepens, and consciousness expands because of my description, as if a star were a crystal on my desk, with gemstones and a glass prism through which I view stars, refracting their colors like words with multiple meanings.

A word can mimic a crystal, and a crystal can describe, also.

5

There's a silver sheen on the land; we don't call it beauty as such, feeling a part of it.

My thought and stars, sisters, splinter into shards that tinkle to the ground and shine.

I notice some thoughts encode meaning in ordinary reality and feeling in the non-ordinary, spirit, rather like footnotes for later.

I speak of our origin in present tense, because sky is circular from here.

Time is not an enclosure or setting for experience.

Relation as place is cyclical between our mesa and the dark net stars shine through, like a black moonstone.

All times continually turn in all superpositions, so space and experience are concentric.

Even though matter and radiance had decoupled, the universe became transparent light filling space.

Two hawks hover above a rocky outcrop shaped like a whale, a resemblance I've noticed before on my walks.

I imagine I'm inside the whale and experience communication between rocks and whales, and I think of other animals illustrated by stars.

Later, I'm told the cosmos communicates with itself through this web of images we imagine.

My attempt at rendering the background imagery.

Human beings are hunched upward and downstream like bright birds.

You believe your are souls of invisible importance.

Mistakes come: our minds open. A wet stream of stuttering clicks and whistles.

It is sort of just my body that has to hear you — a strange sensation that can be made a refuge, even, in much a land. I don't pretend as anyone were still with it sitting...

One sister Olivia, for example, tells me there's a kinship between humans and other beings — it is described...

A deeper-level love I once and believed to love one another...

I feel our love for the friend I find it hard to see. Only the type of the great forget — the friend of its ancestors in the future and every one so overjoyed.

She loves like a tractor of lips and dripping around pink sunblossoms burning...

PEGASUS

1

I never doubted the existence of sky beings, sky deities, or any encounters with ETs.

Stories of beings from the stars and of cosmic travel merge to characterize me as their listener.

I take each subject for her word, during the length of our conversation, and do not ask for evidence.

Though the words aren't unique, they're sincere, and her experiences as such are primary data, in some cases comprising revelation:

One visitor disguised as a primrose teaches my interviewee to ensoul her words with the emotions of flowers.

Dragonflies encircle her, confirming the presence of others, who tell her to plant trees under starlight.

2

Stars are not separate entities lost to each other in the depths of space.

They collect in vast ecologies, galaxies, in an interstellar medium of gas and dust, soil from which to grow.

Gravity contracts the medium, heating it until nuclei fuse, and a new star bursts into light.

At death, huge, old stars consisting now of carbon, oxygen, and iron needed for life explode, returning mass to the medium, then contract into black holes that generate hydrogen for us.

So, matter on earth was made in stars and scattered through space by star explosions.

So, all particles in the universe are entangled.

This state persists until measured by a conscious imagination as experience.

3

Stars demonstrate entanglement by helping us to hold, to integrate light.

The more we restore our relations with stars, the more luminosity.

There's a shift now, as humans seek coherence, this beauty, through imagination.

Star-human communication occurs in mind first, then a way is prepared for contact.

She tells them her hopes, which they amplify; beings align with her thought through an inner connection to their common source.

Imagining may be my perception of hope, and wonder at night sky authenticates contact.

We who watch stars claim the Vital Principal, cosmos, is conscious, minded and intelligent like DNA, plants, stars, evolution.

You could say imagining has the point-like characteristic of creation.

4

There may be an invisible matrix to which artists are drawn via frequencies from other beings, dolphins, for example.

Reality may be a communal construct with these beings.

Through imagining, a co-created small anomaly may start to resonate with higher truth and gradually pervade all around us in widening circles of ET communication.

I wonder if dolphins also swim through inner space to converse with entities there.

What travels is atmosphere, aura, double, and the mind flies instantly through distance, through matter, and significance is a form of telepathy.

ET contact is like consciousness inner space projects upon, until there's enough information to materialize.

Ask a star or planet to come into empty space inside you.

It wishes to contact the other, whom you dream, and to take on this role.

Its contours merge with the dream; estrangements heal.

So you describe the dream as our collectivity with stars and use its synergy for new, hybrid culture.

Few ever see space visitors in their true form as "little people."

They masquerade as colorful rocks, mosses, butterflies, but love most to impersonate iguanas in ruins.

Without imagining, you could walk by and never realize you've seen the Aluxes.

5

We live in relation fields of stars to flowers, to crystals, to star-human exchange.

ETs are neither real nor unreal.

That would be putting the cart in front of the horse, they laugh!

Then Pegasus canters down, so willing to conjoin with us to move forward, so intelligent and kind.

Shamans study astronomy, and yet they call starlight spirit, their gloss for a complexity of occurrence that's non-causal, non-sequential, that happens as it's felt.

Passing in and out of form, beings of waves co-create with us an illumination for consciousness to inhabit.

The matrix of light is like a human body, and psyche is a place.

Whether we come from the stars or from earth, we call stars "ancestors" out of respect.

We connect by their light entering our eyes, and through our bodies we transcribe them.

YOU ARE HERE

1

We've powerful analytic tools to simplify an experience, so we can absorb it emotionally.

There's joy in transmuting a supernova into science and wonder, at the same time.

World's a net of relations in which appearance is one; to correlate the visible with the personal makes it real.

Seeing, a kind of consciousness, materializes form.

Then everything constellates out to the farthest star.

2

So that a family's entangled.

Here is the relation under scrutiny; *there*, yourself as observer, your perceptions, feelings, also everything that is not them.

This quantum state is a property of the boundary or interface separating family, relation, from universe including yourself, because observing leaves you out.

Yet there must be some leakage of information between you.

Imagine a grain of sand beside a rock poised on a ledge.

How does one know of the other's existence?

Then an atom in sand releases a particle that touches the rock, and it falls off the edge.

There must surely be some record of sand in the rock, as of observer in the environment.

Our units of existence are not particles, but exchange, events, context in which attributes are defined by relation, by others.

The measuring device may be an all-seeing universe, and the context intimacy.

3

Now imagine a boundary around the night sky and describe what we'd see, if we looked through it from without.

The limit of information contained there is its total entropy at creation, like a black hole.

All of space emerges as an approximate description or average of how things organize and connect.

A star's temperature is such an average heat of a vast number of moving molecules.

Does that mean coherence, world, is not defined within space-time?

Organization exists not "in" space, its overall geometry, but at the particle level of entwining processes, I mean entities.

Space is a stand-in for complexities of relations among "things" that happen.

Time is relation, i.e., change, but there's a deeper level where time and change are averaged, so we can record any event for later.

The synthesis, recollection, leads inward, since imagining precedes space-time; it has point-source characteristics; it's all at once.

I became very emotional when I realized particles of my body are entangled with every person I've ever known, touched or thought of, not only family, but our president, every artist I've seen or read, strangers described to me by others or named in their prayers.

4

If properties of a thing are just aspects of its relations, can I describe it without reference to time or space?

Does interaction determine how two particles differ, or are particles and forces different manifestations of one body articulated by relation, by contingency?

The description of an object includes every particle or frequency with which it interacts, so we who observe night sky belong to it inextricably.

Rather than mapping it with an arrow pointing to earth, YOU ARE HERE, draw the brightest stars you see with sufficient detail, so there's no other observer, place or moment for which this description would be the same, and even though any description of sky incorporates all beloveds in a hyper-dimensional collectivity of earth and space, data from past and future, consciousness and oversoul, love merging with a star, so you go there.

We say perceptions by different collectivities harmonize by recognizing you, the outsider, as entangling space-time.

It's how to hold "agapē, universal love" in your mind, leaving earth physically and joining the inner collectivity at the same time.

Signed with love: The Entelechy.

LISTENING

1

I'm at my desk on the cove, when suddenly there's presence in inner space.

My words have deeper meaning, well-being, and expand to illuminate the space.

I look up; dolphins are swimming by!

I feel their gladness as they pass back and forth in front of me, puffs of breath into our common air.

Something good is happening to them.

There's little difference between energy inside a dolphin and without.

It's how land balances sky, when matter and spirit are less separate at dusk; I look west to Blue Hill, and Venus rises behind me in the east.

Dark, zigzag horizon of low mountains, Blue Hill, Cadillac, Sargent against cobalt air.

Each projects my line of sight upward, then is lost in a jumble of stars; how to extend a line and retain the landmark's weight, import?

The intersection of dolphin grids on earth and in the sky is inner space.

Awareness, immanence is feeling I can move into their world.

Our neighbor laments, and a vector extends from her emptiness to our compassion for her.

2

I mean this vacuum of twilight is like listening.

I hear a cacophony and try to nurture what's made visible by sound, as by other beings interweaving above the cove.

Fine lines connect dolphin calls; persons and events integrate.

Wavelets, seabirds, wind in pines transmute into a series of gestalts, music eliciting common space.

To communicate with dolphins, understand this shapeshift of sound, for they exist in other space; their frequencies are more rapid, and they interpenetrate with our emotions, as if the beloved were literally within.

Our hope for her collates spirit with this consensus place where water's alive with vibration, and light responds to latencies in the whole, including movements of others, emotion of the author, glacial geology of a cove, heliacal rise and set of Venus, photonic non-materiality of information as empathy.

3

Inner space and world give rise to each other, photon and wave; a person alone is in a context.

It's how a painting, real in itself, also reveals reality by connecting a blue scarf with a woman's blue eyes, for example.

The whole attains to unconcealment, and emotion's the fuel.

Coherence is fueled by awareness, wherein consciousness is the total potential of the vacuum, I mean poised, directed toward greater orders of relation in a painting, as of the capacity for a live system to spontaneously connect outward in beauty.

Inner space is a whirlpool fed by energy running through it, like dolphin benevolence, trust, continuous relation, light and sound of a wave possessing definite mass, charge, spin and so on, but it's indeterminate which particle possesses which attributes, since these constantly change for the whole.

4

A young dolphin receives this swirl of information stepped down from galaxies as vibration, electricity, weather, ambient emotion from meeting and melding with others; she's part of the joyous multiverse; each world's a shapeshift of her experience.

She's loved, and that love is intrinsic; absence merges with open space; everything's held.

Don't blame our friend or wish events otherwise entangled.

Look up at supernovae of limitless fusion driving the exchange of gravity for coherence, as we shift from Newton to quantum.

You shift into gold on water at the end of day; a day can change shape, also.

You may by relation, wave continuity, illuminate a complex and dark context; grace can unfold with your perception of shoreline, horizon.

When the dolphins left, my heartbeat became erratic, and it hurt.

I went out to film our cove in the dark, and a ball of light appeared on my phone, zipping through the beech trees.

Coda

Dawn refers to the time when sky lightens and the space lighted.

Venus, any bright object before sunrise refers to dawn, eliciting a context for inner space that was empty and place, where we deepen our reception to twilight, also.

I breathe in space lit by sunset and breathe out to any star; our compassion draws volume into the vacuum.

Joining trust with compassion to elicit space is a form of divination, like finding a lost person by the arc of a falling star.

My line of sight can leap from mountain to Milky Way, through dark constellations, dense clouds of dust in Andromeda, from day rainbows to black rainbows at night.

When Pray's Meadow Brook flowing into our cove mirrors the Milky Way, poise is expressed.

LUX

1

She does not distinguish spirit from body, which interweave via the senses.

"It begins with wonder, then interest."

The light of mind and sunlight entwine in your eye, though separately each is unseen, like starlight without an object to fall on.

Deep space is black.

Inner life coalesces with daylight, a spectrum on which fluctuations of light from the object stimulate sight, while you simultaneously enhance your reception, until finally you see the ideal within the real.

Your consciousness lovingly assimilates new events to enhance cognition that ensouls space.

I present physical evidence where applicable, but my interest is in my informant and her words.

I learn more about that Eureka moment, when intense phenomenon becomes transparent to the ideal.

2

Material and imaginary flow into each other through a crack of light, "observation," between worlds.

Juxtaposition becomes a blend of unconscious and external event; the more distant the relation, the more emotional, poetic, the perception.

For my witness, bright physical light weakens the interpretive.

But there are two emanations, one from the eye, close to mind, and one from a star, which conjoin.

A close encounter inscribes such diffuse, liminal boundaries of the imaginary.

Psyche becomes increasingly collective, as it assimilates with the gorgeous world.

It's as if a star offered you the nourishing, ineffable light of a new realism between subject and object.

That beings from outer space manifest to you physically is unproven in my field, but still true.

Each account is recorded as fact in my notebook.

Then I can travel up through light and become more intimate with its star.

3

I wake and see out the window a ball of light swirling above the trees.

A woman stands under the trees, where certain plants grow; she knots leaves into a symbol using streamers of light, and as I watch, I know I'll remember.

My window is the same as light going through it; luminous is a better word than translucent.

When I try to describe her, I draw a star; I saw stars like children's stickers on the window glass; I know if I draw one, I can go there.

Darkness is light's resting state in deep space; transparence can occur all at once, the way your face lights with understanding, or a wave passes you to Andromeda with the swiftness of near and far at the same time.

Consciousness may be such a light source with metaphoric power; thread is a feeling of spiritual connection, sunlight is love.

Language and energy interchange; we can experience a physical event by association, algorithm.

A star visitor could be the attribute of such association.

Seeing starlight is seeing the visible in the invisible, that fragile imaginal cloth holding planet and existence together.

When I ask if they're literally extraterrestrials or a metaphor from inner realms, she says there's no difference in significance.

4

Their skies are full of life.

She describes starlight as scalar, without properties of distance or time.

Any spirit in matter she calls starwalking: remote viewing, meditation, intuition, plants she was shown, and any soul possessing a certain shine she calls starlight.

The power of relation came through their extraordinary yellow eyes, she tells me.

You're looking into a star, convex, immense, flashing colors through opalescent, flowing nuclear fusion.

I feel separated from home now; I look up at night sky with great longing.

They showed me earth through their eyes; their oneness extends to us.

Whereas, I'm in the dark; then it opens onto luminescence; there's a lot of "snow."

There's a lot of stars, huge, no horizon and very bright.

I see the Pleiades; I feel like a wolf looking toward home.

Whew! a shooting star just dropped there onto snow, so I go over to it.

A crystal has dropped on the snow, and there's light, a face in the stone; it's as if I'm looking up through the sky and things are very clear, and I'm coming up through the ice.

I've been below all this time, and now I see stars.

DARKNESS

1

Light remains whole, but our understanding of what's elemental changes.

We thought smallest, most indivisible, was fundamental.

Perhaps for light, it's not in smallness, but wholeness of particle and wave.

We no longer measure a single photon moving through space with its attributes.

An attribute is somehow shared property now, of a new kind of object, the whole.

Myriad superpositions replace a photon's trajectory; the entangled one, no longer "traveling," is both here and there.

So darkness may be a more subtly structured fullness of light, the blue vault of day, for example, where darkness passes through air that reflects it.

Dark air is opaque to him, but when I turn on a light, it's transparent.

For him, light activates transparence, the way fire changes the state of air.

Light is a condition of the medium; it's not elemental, is how he explains its invisibility.

2

He presses a smoky quartz to his forehead to see in the dark and to see through objects that by day seem opaque.

Darkness is a better medium for identifying entities; it eliminates confusion with ordinary images of day, for which night sky is often just a foil or metaphor.

Once our daughter locates the Milky Way, we point further out to Andromeda, blur of a trillion stars.

Her seeing opens in psychic congruence with the galaxy, connecting wonder and space to one source.

3

Looking into polar dark night: bright stars and planets, red, blue, green scintillations above, silver sheen on the land.

We don't say beauty as such, due to its abstraction, but feel part of her presence as we walk across the snow, whereas by day, objects are known by their components, and wholeness seems derived, subjunctive.

Comparing a star being to an angel reveals this context for constellations, extraterrestrials, conversations with animals.

You internalize space and ignite a photonic grid so bright as to be darkness to your untrained eyes.

When we enter into that closeness and unboundedness, it feels like disintegration, like everywhere.

A particle, even an association can flash into being, dissolve, then flash over there.

Where previously, vacuum meant empty; now it's invisible, mobile energy; every point in space contains intersecting light from every star.

Context permeates universe, pulsing through dark as information-like creativity, like first space rushing into existence, flinging stars apart.

4

Subtle, entangled, the gestalt I speak of is between myself and an angel.

Energy in matter is precisely balanced by this potential in light and dark, a zero sum.

When experienced as complements of mass-motion, intention-observation, dark matter-dark energy, the void comes into form, intelligibility.

Joy at connecting to this source is expressed by our star's extravagant giveaway of light.

Even darkness generates light when waves move into phase.

Consciousness may be this potential fundamental; it may be the vacuum itself, i.e., aware, directed toward greater coherence, sharing matter-in-relation with dark ground as entropy, breakdown, star dust.

An ET visitation restructures natural law, grace, to manifest its presence of blinding intensity.

Exaltation is a common aftereffect, not part of the recovery process of the abductee for whom cosmic force was perceived as love.

Many spend the rest of their lives helping others.

WONDER

1

One summer night, walking from our house after dinner, stars make the sky almost white.

My awe is like blindness; wonder exchanges for sight.

Star by star comprises a multiplicity like thought, but quiet, too dense for any dark planet between.

While single stars are a feature of the horizon at dusk, caught at the edge of the net of gems.

Transparence hanging on its outer connectedness casts occurrence as accretion, filling in, of extravagant, euphoric blooming.

Then, being as spirit and in matter is known, here to there.

I go home and tell my children to come out and look.

The souls of my two children fly up like little birds into branches of the Milky Way, chatting with each other, naming constellations, comparing crystals and fire.

They exclaim at similarities between what they see in the sky and on our land.

So, by wonder, they strengthen correspondence between sky and home.

Earth is made from this alchemy of all children, human and animal, combined with our deep gratitude.

2

I see his dark shape, moving and shifting against night's screen of stars.

My little girl reaches for his lighted silhouette.

Human beings are thought upward and flown through by bright birds.

We believe stars are spirits of very high frequency.

We feel proud our animals come from stars so dense in meaning close to sacrament.

We describe passing time in stories about animals; star movement is named for seasonal migrations of deer, wolf, hummingbird, dolphin, and as animals stars still walk among us.

Our snake Olivia, for example, tells me there's no conflict between humans and rain, because resource is all around us.

A coyote loved night, and he loved to gaze at the stars.

"I noticed one star in Cassiopeia; I talked to her, and each night she grew brighter and closer until she came to life here, as a corn snake, my friend."

"She looks like a dancer on tiptoe, stepping around pink star-blossoms surging up after rain."

3

Constellations are experienced emotionally as this play of self through plant and animal symbols and values.

A dream atmosphere flows; everything represented is sacred; being moves in accord, not of time.

Returning from the Milky Way, she realized crystals had fallen from her bag and looked up.

My story links a journey to sky with the creation of stars, in which place accommodates becoming.

Chama River flows north-south to the horizon, then straight up through the Milky Way, like water moving beneath a riverbed that's dry.

Abiquiu Mountain, El Rito Creek, coyote, snake, rainbow and rain, spider and hummingbird identify equivalent spiritual placements above, so wherever we go, there is company, nurture, from every star in our regard.

4

I start up to ask my birds to return home, and find our land continuous with a starry sky mapped as entities who set into motion occurrence, here.

Place awaits an imprint from this potential, even though starlight arriving now already happened; what happens is a depth of field, before and after drought, fire, storm disruption.

I move at high speed, but I'm still standing beside my house in the dark.

To go there, I find the place on our mesa that correlates to their tree in the sky and leap up.

Space stirs as star trilliums emerge through darkness like humus.

I ask one blossom to please in the future renew these bonds between sky and my children, so they will always hold light in the minerals of their eyes.

5

Sun on its nightly underground journey weaves a black thread between white days on the cosmic loom, like a cord or resonance between new experience and meaning.

The origin of stars expresses the underlying warp of this fabric; summer solstice draws a diagonal across my floor, precession, weaving ground of informing spirit, so therefore, life is fundamental to stars.

The reverse is well known.

That's why I don't use a telescope, star charts or glasses when I go out; I think of a place; I wait, then fly to my children.

When the star-gate is raised, there's a narrow door between sky and ground.

But when I arrive, I find the sky solid; I can't break through to visit my starbirds and stand there wondering, before dawn.

Then sky vault lifts; maybe I can slip through to find the Milky Way and see its blossoms.

Then our sun appears in the crack and pushes through to the day.

It's so bright, so hot, I step back and cover my eyes; I hear my mother calling.

HEART

1

We felt tired; there were physical ailments.

I notice you're forgetful; you live in the moment.

I don't know what day it is, when you leave for New York, faces, subjects of my poems.

I remove information that no longer serves me in the present.

It's a mix of freedom and loneliness, and the loneliness is like space, so I look up at night sky.

I see Sirius and try to communicate my emotion to a star, and the information moves upward.

Feeling utilizes a conscious grid connecting our sun with other stars, flowing along spiral nebulae; then Sirius becomes intrinsic, close, too bright to see all at once.

All night, I feel subtle energy as stars reflect back the love I've given others.

Photons flow into my eyes and transmute to my own cellular structure.

"Come out and stand with me;" you appear all at once, the way a window appears when I wake.

2

There are fewer people, and I want them to be different.

I don't like one's values or my feelings get hurt; there's a miasm of wounds from childhood.

Pain is a vibration; allow it to shine out as part of your content; it's not consciousness itself.

That substantive light-principle has as many sparks as stars in the cosmos.

You hum with its energy, and as you read, it's merging with others around us.

To visualize a body, look up at cells of energy scattering through the vacuum of night.

I recognize the center of black empyrean is a point in my heart; I can see in the dark, using heart cognition.

You appear all at once, as if opening my eyes I see a window, because your body's transparent.

I see stars and a tiny galaxy through you, as if through my own heart I perceive images you feel, even if you're in New York or Peru.

Place loses its bindings and streams out in ribbons of light.

3

People below move gently across my diffuse, remote peripheries.

The roots of plants and trees show through dimly lit soil.

I can see their sap flow.

A man strolls down Higgins Farm Road, and a white-tail deer leisurely approaches him.

Even around a turn in the road, I see them clearly.

Unifying vision alternates with physical contingency to create the scene.

Space as seeing envelopes island, continent, earth, solar system, galaxy in a floating universe that's gently luminous, like a city from afar.

Stars arrayed in constellations dissolve into scrims of diaphanous flame in white dark; each star is a point source, like the interior star.

4

Light and dark can manifest as one singularity.

Need within may seek a compensatory balance between them, as between yourself and every person you've known.

Entropy and love are new information-bearing frequencies, whose words, thoughts, feelings manifest quickly now, by connecting to our experience with adhesive memory-like gravity.

There's concern this intensity will damage human health; the opposite's true; we transmit loving thoughts on these waves, like vascular antennae.

And our cells quicken to stay resonant with earth.

Crystals, plants, animals naturally shift; weather and genetics upload, so your fears will not materialize as such.

5

I receive messages, while stargazing, as evanescent associations of sound, light, feeling and vibrational images.

Data manifests as an expansion of my aura, a kind of generative instability without ground.

I don't judge one person's aggression, one's opacity or the distance between myself and a loved one.

Emptiness, the quantum plenum, is alive, intrinsically dimensional and white with stars.

Suffering as fluctuations of the vacuum passes into it.

So I'm glad for the advice of our friend, an alien resident who runs the B&B in Abiquiu, as we drive in her white truck with her dog.

Using the speed of light, appearance, she reflects underlying coherence, so when I love others "more" than I'm loved, I'm pulled up into the star cloud.

I open my eyes.

Later, thoughts speed like shooting stars too fast to see, like starlight in other frequencies of other heartbeats, to keep information flowing as we feel chaotic, then change.

My heart radiates back to the collective.

"You receive its force and reflect its stars."

SINGING

1

All day, I feel the approach of dolphins; their thoughts are in my mind.

When I swim, my cells attune to them, because ocean's full of vibrations that transmit to water in my body.

It's a repository of primordial data from space; all creatures in water can access the Akasha.

Tones entering my cells transform into feeling, an awareness of two worlds at once.

I send back my thought, picture, feeling, and together we form new vibrations of knowledge that had been dormant in me.

They're here!

I swim out of the cove toward them.

So happy, I hum, and their answering chorus reverberates across water; we know each other.

One dolphin is still, far below me.

Her form takes shape, as she rises silently in bright blue, motionless, sunlit.

Thank you for showing yourself, fulfilling a deep longing within my deep memory.

2

I empty my mind and listen for her reply, which comes as waves of emotion.

A cloud surrounds me; I expand into its stillness and receive tones conveying information very fast.

They teach me to hum, to whistle and sing; sound amplifies my body across open water; even their joyous play has this sensation of creating space, and when they sleep, stars augment their frequencies.

We converse by mind-cell helixes of image and feeling.

Cosmic legacy, cosmic extension imprint holographically on my heart neurons as dolphin empathy.

There are sounds which can stop time, alter surroundings or shift your dimension.

Swimming I lose my sense of place, even physicality and connect with collective love.

They teach me to join my aura with the cosmos by spiraling with me in sound-star tetrahedrons and to love those with whom we merge.

Then being is healing, through innocence, when the animal becomes the teacher.

3

One dolphin swims toward me; I open telepathically and respond.

I practice this method of reflection to contact lifeforms in other space, who are trying however they can to meet us.

Sirius radiates high frequencies to lighten the dark, denser planets.

Dolphins travel to and from such a planet through diagrams like songs on ocean floors.

They wish us to participate in over-lighting the collectivity of souls in our galaxy and ally with them to access the Space Sister-Brotherhood.

Through these planetary vortices, dolphins catalyze starlight to refresh water on earth.

Transference between species is both cellular and holographic, or geometric.

For example, my friend's body is 3D in front and 4D in the back; she exists across dimensions, while appearing so ordinary in her yellow shirt and blue slacks, as we walk to the shore.

"Memory is vibratory, like DNA, condensed light," she volunteers.

"You and I relate through our mutual past on Sirius, in Glastonbury, Santa Fe."

So I repeat their joyous, staccato syllables; I listen to "pod"casts of Noh singers and tune to high pitches the Pleiades use for propulsion into our atmosphere, using the star codes of dolphins.

4

We've attributes in realities we're not aware of.

Dolphins reside in these dimensions, like dreams in oceans.

They swim within magnetic streams of other entities, angels we've invented, others' heavens, cyclic destiny.

I glimpse one jump from its energy band, attracted by my friend's intense aura.

He shows me earth's sister planet replicated by sound as we co-create it by singing, sitting in her yard, gazing at the ocean under pine trees.

There are messages in clouds, in wavelets on granite, cicada and meadowlark calls.

Space travelers materialize morphogenetically from local beauty and merge with us.

They enable travel between time and stars by projecting tones just ahead of the consciousness of the person migrating, the way dolphins pass me so fast, I don't see the bubbles until they're far, out of sight.

1

You may find at the market, a casual comment swerves into the metaphysical with a young man by produce.

He wears a white tee and jeans, ordinary, yet careful about his food.

"Every time I meditate, I begin in space among the stars," he says.

"Many of these beings," he continues, "are not physically 3D, so it's frustrating to describe them."

"I have the impression their silver color comes from within."

"They look at me with tremendous love from almond-shaped eyes."

"There's no sunlight; the whole cloud structure is luminous and the ground crystalline, a lot of purple and blue like twilight."

It's a complex, half inarticulate narrative, perhaps because he feels I won't believe him, yet he's spontaneous.

I don't need to question the reality of his story.

He's sincere.

2

There's more energy now as heat, connectivity, radio waves, WiFi, X-rays and all kinds of interaction.

You operate with higher electrical current inside, which can rejuvenate you physically by the nature of connectivity, moving freely around the body.

Next week, smiling, mid-sentence, "seeing Earth from deep space, blue and alive."

More often now, ETs are discussed at the co-op, also coincidence, spirit molecules, time tunnels and quantum uncertainty, since we're close to the Santa Fe Institute.

I like that he expresses himself to me as a kind of witness in transition.

He's read my work and thinks me more knowledgeable than I am, since my poems aren't true.

"Pleiadeans create new visuals through which I can imagine," he says.

Care is required for witness to resonate energetically with listener, however nonchalant I appear.

The more compassion one has for non-normal experiences of others, the sooner consciousness will shift toward the stars; to him, this means shifting the ethical structure of communicating his narrative.

"I think of myself in a service capacity."

3

"One silvery insect was seven feet tall; I shook his claw and we conversed."

"Sometimes reptiles hoard crystals to send and receive information."

"They can space-travel versions of themselves to us, as snakes."

"Lipids in membranes behave like that, channeling the atmosphere."

At home I write, "The membrane is like a liquid crystal to the sky."

Next week, in line, he's with a beautiful woman with a worn face, who knows me.

She's not well, and wants me to visit and meet their animals.

"They know they don't end when they die," she says; "It's sad they're leaving, but it's voluntary."

"They've relatives on other planets, sentient beings with the right to vote."

"Have you ever watched an animal and suddenly it disappears?" he chips in.

Witnessing involves a significance equivalent to truth.

"The whole idea of visiting another planet, communicating with a being from another world, to me that's spiritual."

4

"When they speak, they subliminally vary certain sounds; I hear words, but their sound carries different meaning to my body."

"Some words I read weren't there when I began."

"'Use these new words, enhanced by your imagining, to allow our dimension to emerge,' they said; 'Imagination stabilizes the shift.'"

In Santa Fe, in Tucson, Lima, La Paz, people see extraterrestrials.

When I step outside, a velvety multitude of moths and insects, transparencies on my screen door, whirls up to the porch light.

Milky Way shines with white clottings and dark rifts, covering ground and trees with phosphorescence.

Comets, asteroids from deep space, planets moving at will contribute to this glamour of wonder.

He shows me how to pull frequency, starlight, down through his body into the ground, and I try it; I'm more open now.

I can carry more light, which fuses with similar energies in mass consciousness.

Earth will radiate this consciousness as a star or sun on horizons of other worlds.

"Let us hold that portal open for you in the form of your little crush on him, of light streaming down, and feel a surrounding new ideal," they speak to me.

"Now imagine you're here, in the Pleiades."

"You wish to give a present to the source, like compassion or rainwater from home."

Early on, I divined that this book already exists in the future.

After all, I thought of it; it's a probability somewhere, complete, on a shelf.

My intention is to consult that future edition and create this one, the original, for you.

CHACO AND OLIVIA

1

Channeling, part of daily experience, is an underrated technique in literature.

It's natural for an artist to receive information from a non-objective source.

New spirits are expressing themselves from new quantum realms.

There are synchronous memories to integrate and ideas, which suddenly emerge.

One part of myself is taking dictation, while one part enjoys a calm, empty day.

How does my body make room for another, who perceives with my senses?

Does she see what I see, or is merging with me a new hybrid world?

Sometimes the entity comes out of love, and you're like a candle flame; versions of yourself are drawn to you; they fly into you, and you transmute.

Others seek "individual" experience, as frequencies rapidly increase on earth.

Many intelligences reveal themselves through animals or plants.

Ask for a grand enhancement of your identity through trust, through living in the moment, as you sit at your desk.

"We wish you to speak with grama grass, quartz crystals in sand, petals of morning glories, white moths, ants, ravens, new cholla leaves, evaporating rain and to receive the knowledge stored in living form by transcribing."

Writing can shift the mechanism of time by changing the record, then changing the event.

2

Imagine multiple helixes connecting virtually at your navel to access this voice, like threads unraveling a celestial heritage.

And don't be misled by glamour from heaven.

You too radiate light to other worlds seeking to know their creation.

Asleep, you may fly to a place without matter that's connected to you, whether you remember in the day.

An insect singing may be your identity there, a momentum, as surrounding energy moves into this sound.

When I see stunning photographs of earth from space, she has the organized, self-contained look of a living being.

Trust that when earth moves, you move in sync.

Days fill with splendor, and earth offers its pristine beauty to the expanding present.

3

Talking to pets opens a conversation with interdimensionals from beyond our galaxy, whom we would not refer to as beings, whom we perceive by vibration; ask your dog about this.

Any soul may distribute itself into a human, a toy poodle, bacteria, an etheric, or quartz crystal.

One ring of Saturn may view its human portion on earth as "an alien" (ha ha) or the one you love comes from a universe where stars are not distant, no longer either hot or dark.

Those formerly referred to as animals love unconditionally, mentoring us.

Chaco began to speak by resonance, and I understood him through resonance, coherence between us.

He retains words from star languages, since he lives in heaven and on earth simultaneously.

A poodle, a pet corn snake may be an aspect of your own soul from the Pleiades; you love unconditionally.

4

Our atmosphere is layered with energetic grids and pathways.

You find a portal by the frequency contingent with another planet's aliveness.

You may land in an empty world, missing the entrance, if you're not tuned to it.

Sacred ruins protect such openings.

Ancients learned astronomy, the calendar, and ethics from star beings who arrived in ships with lights like pearls they described as tones of speech.

Actually, visitors traveled via a spiritual process of loving those at their destination.

When intent aligns with an ardent desire for the well-being of others, this simple, potent decoding associates to good outcomes.

Some will be drawn to Machu Picchu or Uxmal, to artifacts perhaps no one else sees, because a certain inspiration is required for that dimension.

Others believe the regularity of celestial bodies reflects divine order, but order is a contemplative array in the soul.

By loving unconditionally, we participate in its deep structure and fulfill our animal nature.

5

I wake; someone is sitting on my legs; I sit up and open my eyes in the dark, nothing; I reach out and feel someone's face.

He tells me they don't have physical bodies on his star; "I can place my consciousness in any poet or several poets at once."

"To you we're like sparkly star stickers on a wall."

Collective experience is evolutionary, and collective soul is intensifying consciousness.

"'The force of imagination is the dynamic of growth,' I told Coleridge."

"Now, you feel in the dark and meet one who could invent new starlight to cool earth."

Recalling my fear, I see it was misused energy to startle at bats who flew in with him.

"Even asleep in the eaves, we're building high frequency bridges for you to meet others and know creator's light in us all."

"Hey, will bats, frogs, and insects remain here on earth?" I ask

"We intend to remain; earth was so hospitable to us."

Identifying with wild creatures in total darkness penetrates more deeply into our essence than finding them inert, upside down, in the day.

My book describes how communicating with star beings can teach us to continue our world through love and grace, communal grace.

ACKNOWLEDGMENTS

Grateful acknowledgment to *Brooklyn Rail, Chicago Review, Conjunctions, Granta, Lana Turner, Poetry, Symmetries,* and *Tripwire,* where these poems first appeared.

Thank you, friends, authors, and artists who helped me to read and write this book.

Thank you, New Directions.

"Consciousness Self-Learns" is dedicated to Jack Tilton.